Images of EXMOOR

COAST AND COMBE

The pages of this book are dedicated to
the memory of Bryan Parker who, despite his
blindness, enjoyed 'seeing' all our work; and to our
dear friend Annie, who walked every mile with us.

Both now departed.

Front cover photograph: *Porlock Bay*
Back cover photograph: *Thurley Combe*

Images of EXMOOR

COAST AND COMBE

Tim and Caroline Shipsey

EXMOOR BOOKS

First published in Great Britain by Exmoor Books, 1997
Copyright © 1997 Tim and Caroline Shipsey

Original prints are available from:
Little Court Cottage, Grib Lane,
Blagdon, North Somerset
Telephone: 01761 462229

The opinions expressed in this book are those of the authors and are
not necessarily those of the Exmoor National Park Authority

British Library Cataloguing in Publication Data
A Catalogue Record for this book is available from the British Library.

ISBN 0 86183 405 4 (paperback)
ISBN 0 86183 400 3 (hardback)

Exmoor Books
Dulverton Somerset

Trade sales enquiries:
EXMOOR BOOKS
Halsgrove House
Lower Moor Way
Tiverton EX16 6SS
Tel: 01884 243242
Fax: 01884 243325

Exmoor Books is a partnership between
The Exmoor Press and Exmoor National Park Authority

Printed and bound in Italy by Tipolitografia Petruzzi, Corrado + C.

CONTENTS

INTRODUCTION

Exmoor, unlike the other upland areas of the South West, runs directly to the sea. The Bristol Channel – or Severn Sea – curving into the broad Atlantic, has over the centuries been both route for attack and line of defence; a means of escape for the emigrant and a gateway for the tourist; and, above all (at least until the coming of the railway and improved roads), the main artery for trade, in and out.

After the end of the last Ice Age sea level rose rapidly by some 80m-100m, flooding large areas of land on Exmoor's northern edge including the now submerged forests at Porlock Weir and Blue Anchor. At the new limit, the resistance of the rocks to marine erosion produced some of the highest cliffs in England, of the so called 'hogs-back' formation which fall steeply from moor to sea. Until recently the cliffs have been relatively stable. However, in the late twentieth century the increasing frequency of exceptionally high tides along the Channel (which has in any case the highest tidal range in Europe) has resulted in cliff face collapses in many places along the coast as well as the breach of the shingle ridge at Porlock.

The rivers of Exmoor, broadly speaking, rise in the central plateau running from the Chains in the west to the Brendon Hills, in the east. Several, like the mighty Barle and Exe, flow south the many miles to the English Channel. Others take the much shorter journey to the northern coast, including the Pill, Avill, Aller, East Lyn and West Lyn. They fall over 1000 feet within a few miles and, with their tributaries, have carved out steep-sided valleys and combes in their rush to the sea. For most of the time they are placid and picturesque. Occasionally, though, sheer volume of rainfall (for which Exmoor is renowned) can transform them into raging torrents. Exceptionally, as in 1952 when Lynmouth was devastated and other Exmoor communities ravaged, they can wreak havoc and destruction.

Lynmouth, Porlock, Minehead, Dunster and Watchet developed around harbours at the mouth of the high-land rivers as they entered the sea. In time, some became sophisticated with harbour walls, jetties and piers. Minehead and Watchet became important ports, trading as far afield as the continent and Ireland. Minehead was well known as a wool centre, with raw wool, yarn and finished cloth being taken in and out, before declining in the nineteenth century. Watchet's heyday was in Victorian times, when iron ore was brought down from the Brendon Hills and shipped out to the furnaces of South Wales. Watchet was also a centre of paper production and the harbour was able to rely on raw material imports for that industry after the ore trade had ceased. From the 1960s new general shipping activities were developed, but these had foundered by the 1990s and at the close of the millennium Watchet's future seems to depend on the creation of water-related leisure facilities.

Porlock, Lynmouth and other small harbours developed a local trade in coal and foodstuffs, lime as fertilizer for the moorland farms and fishing, particularly for herring. Ilfracombe, at the western tip of the Exmoor coast had grown for somewhat different reasons. Less a trading centre than a refuge and service port for Bristol Channel shipping, in the early 1800s it established a reputation as a fashionable watering hole accessible by sea. The first paddle steamer visited Ilfracombe in 1822, a signal of the growing appeal of the Exmoor coast to the tourist. In time the coming of the railway – to Ilfracombe and Lynmouth from Barnstaple to the south, and Watchet, Dunster and Minehead, from Taunton to the east, and later still motorised transport, killed off the pleasure steamer: the *Waverley* and *Balmoral* are the only regular callers now. But the tourists and trippers, however they came, did so in increasing numbers and a substantial industry arose to cater for them. The smaller coastal resorts like Porlock and Lynmouth, to a large degree depended for their attraction on their small-scale charm. Ilfracombe and Minehead, on the other hand, became typical Victorian seaside towns, replete with large hotels and public promenades. After the Second World War Minehead was chosen as the location of one of Sir Billy Butlin's largest holiday camps – today, re-named Somerwest World, it is the biggest holiday centre in Europe.

A few other industries have taken root on the Exmoor side of the Channel shore, including nuclear power generation at Hinkley Point (which requires millions of gallons of sea water for its turbines). However, the influx of new people and new ideas has not killed off local tradition – indeed, in many respects the interest shown by 'outsiders' has helped to preserve or revive ancient customs. The origins of the Minehead Hobby Horse are lost in the mists of time – possibly deriving from successful attempts to frighten away marauding Danes. Immediately after the War the ceremony entered a bleak period of dwindling support, but it has since regained a widespread following and recognition. The Hunting of the Earl of Rone at Combe Martin is, similarly, a festival whose origins lie so long ago as to have been almost forgotten. Tales abound of the 'Earl' being Lord Tyrone, who according to legend was a traitor shipwrecked on the North Devon coast in the early 1600s, apprehended by soldiers from Barnstaple and despatched to Exeter where he was executed. This story probably has some basis in fact but is more myth than truth. What is clear, however, is that the Hunting of the Earl of Rone was suppressed in the 1830s and only revived in the 1970s, since when it has become again a firm part of the local scene.

That these ceremonies survive and flourish amidst modernity is a reflection of how in Exmoor the past can exist with the present in one distinctive whole. Agriculture on the moor has changed and adapted to meet the national (and now international) market. Coastal trade has given way to seaside tourism. But, like the hog's-back cliffs pounded by the pressures of the sea, Exmoor retains a characteristic identity despite the onslaughts of the late twentieth century. Its mixture of fields and woods, hedgebanks and lanes, heather moor and grass moor, farmsteads, hill villages and seaside towns, can be found in no other part of the kingdom. On the coast as inland, the hand of man has shaped nature over millennia, but has never wholly tamed it. With vigilance, this unique landscape will continue to evolve in ways consistent with its past and to the benefit of its beauty.

AUTHORS' PREFACE

Since 1992 when the first *Images of Exmoor* was published, we have continued to add to our photographic collection of the life and landscape of Exmoor. During the past five years we have extended our interest into places beyond the boundary of the National Park and developed a greater understanding of the area as a whole. Some of the photographs in this book are selected from the period 1987-92, which we were unable to include in the first volume, plus new material taken specifically for this book.

The coastline of West Somerset and North Devon must be one of the most wonderfully varied in the country – from the gentle, sloping shores of Bridgwater Bay to the summit of the Great Hangman at 1043ft (318 metres). The area we cover in the following pages extends from approximately Kilve in Somerset, along the coast to Woolacombe in Devon, taking a look inland at some of the most striking and popular places in between.

The book was originally conceived as a visual journey, illustrating the places the visitor arriving in the area via the A39 would see, including detours off the main road to explore some of the moorland, hills and combes that make up this varied landscape. However, as the book developed it became apparent that there were different ways in which

the coast could be experienced, not just by walking or driving as close as possible to it. In the course of taking these photographs we climbed to the top of hills inland, the view taking in great expanses of countryside extending to the coast, walked the coast path, rode the West Somerset Railway, took boat trips aboard pleasure craft and the paddle steamer *Waverley* and finally took to the air in a helicopter. This combination of viewing experiences enabled us to present a collection of pictures that show what an astonishing mix of coast and countryside lies within quite a small area.

The attraction of Exmoor exists in the complexity of its scenery. From the bleak moorland of the Chains, across heather-covered Dunkery, down into the wooded river valleys of Horner and the Barle, along steep hog's-back cliffs extending from Combe Martin in the west to North Hill in the east , and up to the farming country of the Brendon Hills. All this lies within the 265 square miles of the Exmoor National Park. Add to this the adjoining areas of coast to the east and west and you have an endlessly fascinating landscape, a delight to the photographer, walker or motorist.

The relentless action of the sea at the base of the cliffs and the weathering erosion of the cliff tops contribute to an

unstable and constantly changing coastline. The tell-tale signs can be seen in numerous places along the shore – the fencing that dangles over the cliff edge at Kilve, the new sea defences at Minehead, the flooding of Porlock Marshes, the land slip near Culbone and the various diversions of the South West Coast Path. By contrast the moors and combes have evolved slowly and, apart from seasonal changes, are apparently much the same as when we first visited Exmoor. But they are subject to particular pressures of a different kind – visitor numbers, and agricultural change foremost amongst them. The example of generations of families who shaped the Exmoor landscape, has been followed by their successors today and this has helped significantly to protect the special character of the area. The Exmoor National Park Authority, too, treads carefully the difficult line between exposure and preservation. So we can only echo the hope we expressed in our previous volume: that our photographs will deepen the appreciation of Exmoor and the delicate balance that is necessary for its survival.

Tim and Caroline Shipsey

NORTH

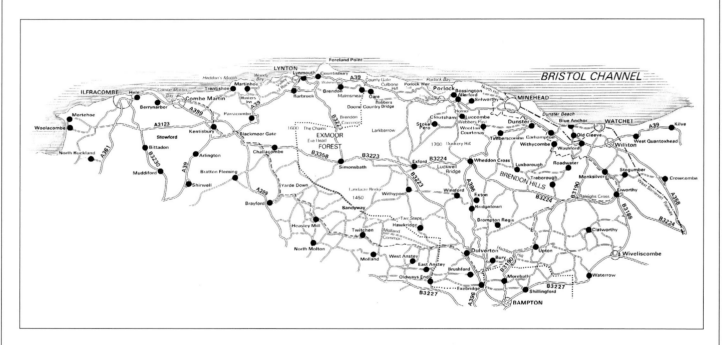

This map was prepared by the Exmoor National Park Authority from aerial survey photography, the copyright being held by the Authority.

E.N.P. Boundary ⎯ ⎯ ⎯ ⎯ ⎯ ⎯

County Boundary ....

Approximate Height in feet

above sea level __1500__

Miles   0   5

Kilometres   0   5

On a summer's day, from the Quantocks above Bicknoller, the view
extends across the Brendon Hills to distant Exmoor and along the coast to
Minehead. This is a landscape of great variety in a comparatively small
area. Ancient woodland, windswept moors and the ever-changing coast
lie together within just a few miles, interspersed with a patchwork of
farmland and picturesque villages.

11

From Quantock's Head toward Blue Ben.

Looking across East Quantoxhead where Court House has been home to
the Luttrell family for many generations.

The *Somerset Year Book* of 1924 reported a 'new
discovery' – oil-bearing shales. Apparently the
beds of oil-rich shales extended from Watchet
to the Parrett estuary, to a depth of 1000ft.
A company was set up and although it did
produce some barrels of oil at Kilve, it ceased
operation in less than a year. All that remains
is a brick built retort regarded with curiosity by
many visitors who know nothing of the industry
that might have destroyed what Coleridge once
described as 'Kilve's delightful shore'. It is
somewhat ironic that industry did come to
this area in the shape of nuclear power at
Hinkley Point.

Hinkley Point power stations emerging from the mist. Electricity has been produced here since 1965. The public are welcome as visitors and free guided tours are available by arrangement; there is also a nature trail with wheelchair access.

Winter sunset from Kilve.

The shores between Kilve and Watchet are a great source of interesting fossils, some of which like this ammonite are quite large.

St Etheldreda's church at St Audries.

From the Brendons near Treborough Common there are fine views of Blue
Anchor Bay and the patchwork of countryside inland.

The cliffs between Helwell Bay and Watchet are rich sources of alabaster
which was mined during the seventeenth century.

Watchet was once a busy and thriving port, the first record of the harbour
being in 1458. Plans are underway for the harbour to be developed as a
marina and so breathe life back into the town.

The town's excellent museum is situated in the Market House adjacent
to the harbour and is well worth a visit.

Soft red sandstone cliffs at Blue Anchor are constantly crumbling
and slipping due to undermining by the sea at their base.

In 1995 rough weather caused this once familiar rock face to fall away.
Massive boulders – some as big as buses – fell to the shore.

✳

As land is taken by the sea, the coastal footpath
is regularly diverted inland. The West Somerset
Railway, which runs from Bishops Lydeard
to Minehead for some 20 miles, provides an
alternative way to experience both coastal
scenery and the gentle countryside. There are
ten restored stations along the route, each with
its own individual character. Both steam and
diesel trains regularly run along the route and
many of the staff are enthusiastic volunteers.

✳

The *City of Truro* steaming towards Williton.

Williton Station.

Iris and Harry Horne at Stogumber.

Bert Blake at Minehead.

The first chalets appeared on Dunster Beach in the late 1920s.
This peaceful holiday village is a haven for the owners who enjoy
both the wildlife and tranquillity of its setting.

Dunster Castle viewed from beneath Conygar Tower. The Castle is now owned by the National Trust. Before that only two families had owned it since it was built sometime in the eleventh century.

Dunster town from the air.

Blenheim Gardens, Minehead are renowned for their beautiful flowers
throughout spring and summer.

Storms have frequently breached the sea wall at Minehead but scenes like
these in October 1996 should not reoccur following the construction of
substantial new defences.

Hobby Horses at Cher Steep.

Over the first three days of May, Hobby Horses visit various parts of Minehead accompanied by musicians and drummers. The familiar tune and drum beat can be heard drifting across the town as the horse cavorts through the streets followed by an enthusiastic throng.

Minehead town. There are fine walks on North Hill which provide
spectacular views of the surrounding countryside from the Quantocks
in the east to Foreland Point in the west.

The Vale of Porlock from Bossington Hill.

The old coast path from Hurlestone Point to Minehead is not
recommended to the walker today. Whilst the scenery is dramatic, in
many places the path is narrow and steep and frankly dangerous.

Selworthy church gleaming brightly, a familiar landmark to many.

Crawter Hill looking across to Dunkery in early morning sunlight.

The farmland of the Holnicote Estate, owned by the National Trust, for
many years home to point-to-point racing. This very popular sport
enjoyed by large crowds each year is run by the local hunts.

After a short climb up Halse Combe the walker can take a choice of paths,
each with its own special charm.

The Horner valley.

Cloutsham Ball as storm clouds break briefly.

The Devon and Somerset Staghounds at Webber's Post.

Porlock enjoys a sheltered position beneath the hills. The steep hill out of
the village was first travelled by a motor car in 1901. Even today it is still
feared by some who prefer to take the scenic toll road.

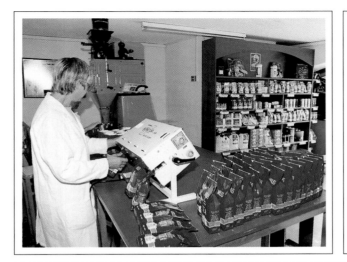

Miles Tea is well known throughout the South West. The family business
has been blending tea and coffee for more than a hundred years and
is based in Porlock. Visitors can buy a wide choice of products from
the well-stocked shop.

The shingle ridge at Porlock Marsh has been breached on a
number of occasions during the past ninety years and the farmland
behind flooded. In October 1996 a most serious breach occurred and
large areas of farmland were lost completely to the sea. Rather than
attempt to hold back the sea it is intended to undertake only limited
intervention work in the future.

Cottages at Porlock Weir back on to the shingle ridge.

The inner harbour at Porlock Weir.

The track from Silcombe Farm is an alternative route to
Culbone church. The coastal path from Porlock Weir is
constantly changing course due to land slips.

Culbone church – the smallest complete church in England nestles in a
wooded combe some 400ft above sea level.

Autumn colours begin to show around Wilmersham Farm.

The peaceful waters of Nutscale reservoir nestle in a steep-sided valley fed
mainly by Chetsford Water.

The view from Spangate in early summer.

From the slopes of Dunkery towards Porlock Common.

Aerial view of Chetsford Water with Honeycombe Hill in the foreground.

Chetsford Bridge and Hurdle Down beyond.

Open moorland at the head of Weir Water.

Brightworthy Barrows in the far distance viewed from Horsen.

The River Barle winds its way between Pickedstones Farm
and Great Ferny Ball.

On the route of the Two Moors Way, Withypool is one of the oldest settlements on the moor.

The ancient clapper bridge at Tarr Steps.

Ilkerton Ridge viewed from South Common.

From Broadmead towards Shoulsbarrow Common.

The Sheep fold at Great Buscombe.

Middle Hill and Cheriton Ridge from Dry Bridge.

The Longstone standing high on the moors between Woodbarrow Gate
and Chapman Barrows.

Weathered by nature – little can withstand the
strong winds on exposed uplands.

Hoaroak Water named after the series of oaks which have for centuries
marked the boundary of the Royal Forest of Exmoor.

At Brendon Two Gates the view across Hoccombe Hill
and Badgworthy Hill.

In June, Paddy cuts peat on Brendon Common
for Dick French of Brendon Barton. Over a
period of seven to ten days the peat will be cut
and laid out to dry. It is left for about fourteen
days then turned and dried for a further seven
days before being stored at the farm as fuel for
both Aga cooker and open fire. The ancient right
of turbary permits the rightholder to cut as
much peat as he can burn on his own hearth.

Badgworthy Hill and Deer Park.

Badgworthy Water forms part of the Devon–Somerset border along its
entire 3 mile length. This is the very heart of Doone Country.

The village of Oare from Deddy Combe.

Oare Church, visited by thousands each year, famous for the shooting of
Lorna Doone on her wedding day in R.D. Blackmore's famous novel.

Glenthorne Estate is private property but there exists a network of
excellent walks and nature trails by agreement with the National Park.

Sugarloaf Hill.

A familiar view towards Brendon from County Gate.

Brendon village hosts an annual Pony Fair in October each year.
The ponies are rounded up from the outlying areas of the moor
and driven down to Brendon Barton.

The number of wild ponies sold is strictly limited and, in order for the event to continue, it is necessary for general farm, household goods and sheep to be auctioned as well.

Long Pool in the East Lyn valley near Rockford.

The Watersmeet area looking across Horners Neck Wood
towards Myrtleberry Cleave.

From the top of Countisbury Hill there are spectacular views
into the East Lyn valley.

Stormy weather over Lynton.

Farmland at Kipscombe.

❋

The dramatic descent of Countisbury Hill affords
spectacular views of the cliffs above Sillery
Sands and leads to Lynmouth, one of Exmoor's
most popular places. There is much to interest
the visitor – a busy harbour which offers fishing
trips, the cliff railway linking Lynton and
Lynmouth, and lovely walks along the West Lyn
Gorge or East Lyn to Watersmeet.

❋

Lynmouth and Lynton. An aerial view, looking inland towards the
Chains. The violent storms of August 1952 that fell on this area caused
loss of life and great damage to Lynmouth.

Overlooking the harbour, the Rising Sun built over six hundred
years ago basks in the sunshine.

Ken Oxenham takes a booking for a fishing trip.

Bob Jones now retired, in the workshop of the Cliff Railway.

The harbour and Rhenish Tower, Lynmouth.

Barbrook, where the raging waters of the West Lyn
destroyed cottages in 1952.

The West Lyn reaches the sea at Lynmouth.

Castle Rock, Valley of the Rocks.

The Valley of the Rocks provides an unusual location for wedding
photographs of Wayne and Sarah.

Lynton and Lynmouth Cricket Club was founded in 1876. The location of its ground in the Valley of the Rocks must surely be one of the most unusual in the country.

Sadly, on 1 April 1997, the pavilion was set alight by vandals and burnt out. Undeterred, the club continues to play and the pavilion will be rebuilt, as close to the original as possible.

North Walk, from Lynton to the Valley of the Rocks, engineered by a
Mr Sanford in 1817. This was described by Thomas Henry Cooper,
writing in 1853, as 'one of the finest terrace walks imaginable'.

Wringcliff Bay, Valley of the Rocks.

Lee Bay. Lee Abbey is a misnomer. The original dwelling was a
farmhouse, upgraded to a small manor house. Only when it was
rebuilt around 1850 was it christened Lee Abbey. As such it
sits dramatically above the bay.

Woody Bay and Valley of the Rocks.

Woody Bay, clad with oak almost to sea level. The old lime kiln and
slipway have been restored by the National Trust which owns 120 acres
of the Woody Bay Manor Estate.

Cliffs between Woody Bay and Heddon's Mouth.

Heddon's Mouth.

The Heddon valley.

Coastline beneath Trentishoe Down.

From Trentishoe Down.

The village of Parracombe is just off the A39 in the Heddon valley. It has
two churches, one of which was built in the nineteenth century replacing
the outlying thirteenth century church dedicated to St Petroc.

Towards Holdstone Down.

The coastline approaching Combe Martin is best viewed from the sea.

Sherrycombe waterfall.

Combe Martin.

Sandy Bay, Combe Martin.

Each year over the Spring Bank Holiday
weekend, come rain or shine, the villagers of
Combe Martin hunt the Earl of Rone.
Depending on the day, the party includes
Grenadiers, a be-ribboned Hobby Horse led by
a broom -wielding Fool in a smock, drummers,
musicians, and a masked person riding back-to-
front on a donkey – the Earl of Rone. You
will see him regularly shot by the Grenadiers,
revived by the Fool and Hobby Horse,
remounted and eventually thrown into
the sea. This extraordinary ceremony
is unique and well worth watching.

From the coast path, looking back to Great Hangman
and Holdstone Down.

Watermouth, with its sheltered harbour. The castle built in 1825 is now a family entertainment centre.

Ilfracombe is the largest holiday resort in North Devon.
Despite having lost some of its Victorian splendour the town is set in
beautiful countryside and has much to offer the visitor.

The harbour hosts boats of all kinds and pleasure steamers
call during summer months.

A new lifeboat house was built in 1996 at Ilfracombe.
Coxswain Andrew Putt who is a full time member of the service,
also serves as mechanic to the *Spirit of Derbyshire* and *Alec Dykes*,
providing both inshore and long distance cover.

The *Spirit of Derbyshire* being manoeuvred to return to the old lifeboat house. Previously the tractor had to negotiate the roads alongside the quay to launch the boat. A slipway is in the course of construction which will enable the boat to be launched directly from the boat house.

Torrs Park and Seven Hills to the west of Ilfracombe.

Rockham Bay has claimed a number of vessels on its treacherous shores.
Bull Point lighthouse was built in 1879 as a warning beacon to mariners.

Mortehoe basks in morning sunshine with Lundy island
just visible in the distance.

The golden sands of Woolacombe stretch for some 3 miles, a welcome
contrast to the stony beaches of the surrounding area.

✳

The end of our photographic journey,
and a return to Bossington Hill with the sun
setting over the Foreland Point.

✳

ACKNOWLEDGEMENTS

Our thanks go to those who have inspired and encouraged us over recent years, particularly the people of Exmoor. The friendships made have sustained us through some difficult times and we thank them all.

Our special thanks go to Diana and Maurice Scott, Pam and Mike Williams of Porlock, Dick and Lorna French of Brendon Barton, Pat and Paul Hartley of Combe Martin and Karen Binaccioni our designer at Exmoor Books.